Skipingo Home

Library of Congress Control Number: 2008934275

ISBN 978-1-58150-205-3

Printed in China
First Edition: 2008

EP
ECLIPSE
PRESS

a division of
Blood-Horse Publications
PUBLISHERS SINCE 1916

*S*kipingo Home

JANE LYON AND KAREN BAILEY

ILLUSTRATIONS BY SUSIE GORDON

The first thing I remember, on the night I was born,

The evening was cold, but the girl's touch was warm.

My front legs were bent and I barely could stand,

So she stayed in my stall to lend me a hand.

My mom was her favorite, a brave little gray,

Who produced many foals and was called Ingot Way.

We lived a wonderful life on Summer Wind Farm,

In lush bluegrass fields. Our life seemed charmed.

I soon learned my family was all bred to run,
As I frolicked and played in the bright Bluegrass sun.
I ran with my mother and raced with my friends,
Through great rolling pastures for days without end!

My brother was famous, the champ of his day,

A big silver stallion they called SKIP AWAY.

He won many races and was Horse of the Year!

To follow in those hoofprints was something to fear.

My name was chosen, my bloodlines to show,
So the plaque on my halter was spelled SKIPINGO

The girl always told me, "You're special, too!"

And she loved me and praised me, as slowly I grew.

Susie Gordon

Time passes quickly when you're having fun,

And it soon was the summer of the year I turned one.

Then came the sales ... I was led into the ring,

I was bought by a prince, the son of a king!

There were tears in her eyes as they took me away,

But the girl said, "Don't worry, I'll find you some day."

They put me in training to learn
how to race,
     Though I tried really hard,
I was rarely first place.
     I thought it would be easy to run
like my kin,
     But of all the racehorses,
just a few ever win.

I was shuffled around for nearly five years,

To run for small purses with lower-class peers.

Each time I lost, a little spark died,

Where there used to be hope, I was hollow inside.

One day the prince died, although not very old,

And it was decided that I would be sold.

Nobody wants an old horse who can't run,

And I really believed that my life was near done.

Back at the sales, alone in my stall,

I wondered if I'd be remembered at all.

Then I heard a voice, my heart gave a leap!

It seemed that the girl had a promise to keep.

Someone did want me, and called me her friend,

She took me back, to beloved Summer Wind!

With the sun on my withers and good feed in my stall,
I began to believe in myself, after all.

With patience and love, the girl taught me to jump.

I can clear all the fences, with rarely a bump!

We're not all so lucky, so I never will roam,

And this story is ending with — SKIPINGO HOME!

EPILOGUE

The last time you saw me, my life was all new.

Now, just a few years later, I'm a champion too!

SKIPINGO'S STORY

A YEAR BEFORE SKIP AWAY WON the 1997 Breeders' Cup Classic to become Horse of the Year, Summer Wind Farm bought his mother at the Keeneland November sale. Ingot Way was carrying a full brother to the champion.

Skipingo was born at Summer Wind on April 26, 1997. Unlike his famous gray brother, the colt was a bay. He quickly became a favorite of farm owner Jane Lyon and her daughter Karen Bailey, Summer Wind's broodmare manager.

Though Jane and Karen had a soft spot for Skipingo, as commercial breeders they resolved to sell him at the Keeneland yearling sale along with other young horses they raised. Skipingo's bloodlines caught the attention of Prince Ahmed bin Salman, who owned a successful racing stable in the United States. The prince bought the yearling and sent him to be trained.

Despite his bloodlines, Skipingo did not shine on the racetrack. In his first year of racing, he did not win at all. The next year, as a three-year-old, he managed to win twice — but no more in two subsequent seasons.

After Prince Salman's death in 2004, his estate sent Skipingo back to Keeneland to be sold. Karen Bailey spotted the now seven-year-old horse and bought him for a modest $4,500.

She took Skipingo home, taught him how to jump, and has enjoyed his winning ways in the show ring ever since.

KAREN BAILEY

JANE LYON AND

JANE LYON is living her lifelong dream of raising Thoroughbreds in the bluegrass of Kentucky. An avid animal lover, she and her daughter **KAREN BAILEY** are intimately involved in every aspect of the family's Summer Wind Farm near Georgetown and are dedicated to equine

KAREN BAILEY

welfare. Jane has written poetry for years, but *Skipingo Home* is her first book. Karen is an accomplished hunter-jumper rider and a licensed wildlife rehabilitator.

Part of the proceeds of *Skipingo Home* will go to organizations that promote Thoroughbred rescue.

Susie Gordon

THE SOFT YET DETAILED DRAWINGS of Susie Gordon add a realistic touch to the children's book *Skipingo Home* and the story it tells about a racehorse given a second chance. Complete with a tint of color, the drawings subtly show how "things really look," according to Gordon.

Although children's book illustration is new to Gordon, she is a longtime artist known for her love of animals, including the horse. She is a frequent exhibitor at the American Academy of Equine Art's fall show and exhibition.

Gordon was trained at the acclaimed Columbus College of Art and Design, where she worked in fine art painting and lost wax bronze, and at the Beartooth School of Art, where she trained with Carl Brenders. Her work, including the award-winning tiger painting, *Behold*, recently was offered to the public.

Gordon lives in North Lewisburg, Ohio, with her husband, Eric, and children, Tristan, Miriam, and Landon. Among the numerous animals she counts as family are Welsh Mountain ponies, Arabian horses, a Friesian mare, Scottish deerhounds, a border collie, and a schipperke.